Libra

THIS BOOK BELONGS TO:

_____

THE WONDERFUL WORLD OF ZODIACS

Mimi Jones

Dedicated to all the knowledge seekers.

All rights reserved.
No part of this book may be reproduced in any form or by any means, electronic or mechanical, and no photocopying or recording, unless you have written permission from the author.

ISBN 978-1-958985-54-0

Text copyright © 2025 by Mimi Jones

www.joeysavestheday.com

A Mimi Book

WELCOME TO: THE WONDERFUL WORLD OF ZODIACS

LIBRA

Mimi Jones

Dates:

Libra spans from September 23 to October 22.

Element:
Libra is an Air sign.

CANCER

Ruling Planet:

Venus rules Libra.

Symbol:

The Scales represent Libra.

LIBRA

Personality:

Libras are known for being diplomatic and sociable.

Strength:

They are very fair-minded and charming.

♎ CHARMING ♎

Color:

Their lucky colors are pink, blue, and pastel shades.

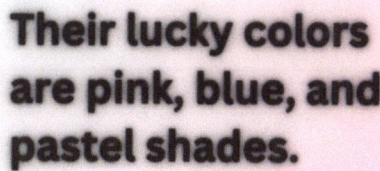

Lucky Numbers:

6, 9, 15, and 24 are lucky for Libras.

Compatibility:

Libra gets along well with Gemini, Aquarius, Leo, and Sagittarius.

GEMINI

AQUARIUS

LEO

SAGITTARIUS

Likes:

Libras love balance, beauty, and meaningful connections.

Career:

They excel in careers that require creativity and collaboration.

Negative Trait:

Sometimes, they can be overly idealistic.

Libra

Motto:

Their motto is "I balance.

Health:

Libras should take care of their kidneys and lower back.

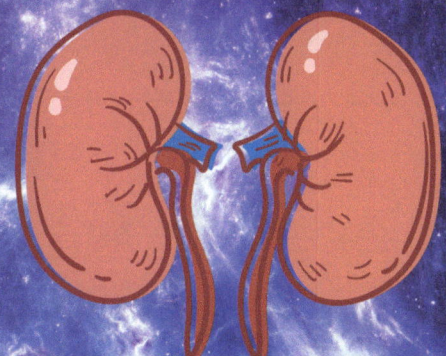
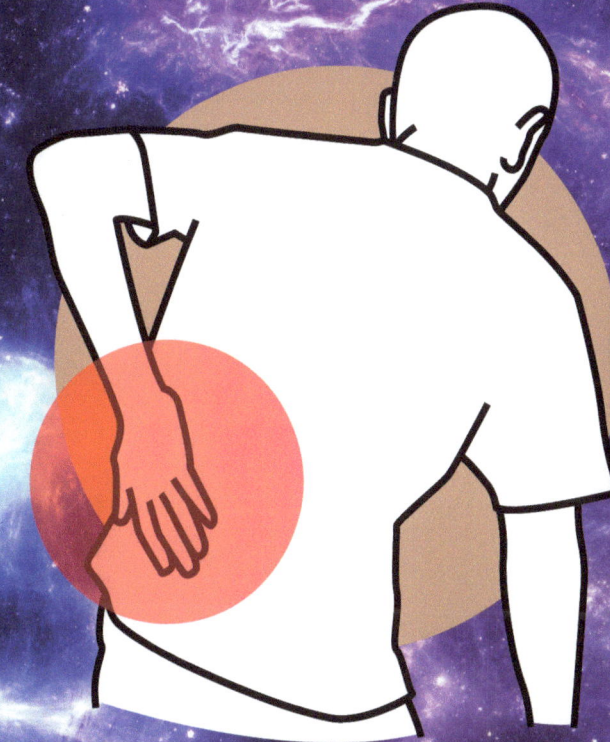

Explore the Possibilities

Hobbies:

They enjoy decorating, socializing, and exploring art.

Libra

Famous Libras:

Some famous Libras include Amiri Baraka, Marina Tsvetaeva, and T. S. Eliot.

Challenges:

Libras need to learn to make firm decisions and face conflict when necessary.

Friendship:

They are friendly and diplomatic friends who can mediate any dispute.

Love Life:

In relationships, Libras are romantic and devoted to harmony.

LIBRA

Influence:
They inspire others with their charm and sense of fairness.

INSPIRE OTHERS

Favorite Activities:

Libras love activities that involve socializing and aesthetics.

Symbolic Object:

The Scales symbolize their quest for balance and justice.

Birthstones:

Opal and sapphire.

If this Zodiac gem tickled your celestial fancy, then you're in for a treat! Dive into my other Zodiac delights right here:

www.mimibooks.com

THE END!

www.ingramcontent.com/pod-product-compliance
Lightning Source LLC
Chambersburg PA
CBHW040030050426
42453CB00002B/66